boilerplate MW01147652

SHORT PLAYS AND MONOLOGUES

BY DAVID MAMET

DRAMATISTS
PLAY SERVICE
INC.

These pieces were written variously as curtain raisers for other plays of mine, as cabaret pieces, and as experiments. PRAIRIE DU CHIEN was originally a radio drama. They were written to be performed on a bare stage, using only a chair or two, and without props or special costuming.

CONTENTS

The Blue Hour: City Sketches

THE BLUE HOUR was first performed as a workshop at the Public Theatre. The actors were Ben Halley, Jr.; David Sabin; Arthur French; Patti Lupone; José Santana; and Lindsay Crouse. The workshop was directed by the author.

CHARACTERS

Prologue: American Twilight . . . . MAN

Doctor . . . . DOCTOR
WOMAN

The Hat . . . . CUSTOMER
SALESWOMAN

Businessmen . . . . GREY
BLACK

Cold . . . . A
B

Epilogue . . . . MAN

6

The Blue Hour: City Sketches

PROLOGUE: AMERICAN TWILIGHT

MAN. In great American cities at *l'heure bleu* airborne dust particles cause buildings to appear lightly outlined in black. The people hurry home. They take a taxi or they walk or crush into the elevated trains or subways; or they go into the library where it is open and sit down and read a magazine and wait a bit so that the crush of travelers will dissipate.

This is the Blue Hour.

The sky is blue and people feel blue.

When they look up they will see a light or "powder" blue is in the Western sky where, meanwhile, in the East the sky is midnight blue; and this shade creeps up to the zenith and beyond, and changes powder blue to midnight and, eventually, to black, whereat the buildings lose their outlines and become as stageflats in the glow of incandescent lamps. This is the Blue Hour—the American twilight as it falls today in the cities.

DOCTOR

DOCTOR. Now, what seems to be your problem?

WOMAN. I won't pay this. (*Waves bill.*)

DOCTOR. Won't pay what, I'm sorry.

WOMAN. I won't pay this.

DOCTOR. Well, let's see what it is. (*Takes bill.*) Now, what's the problem here?

WOMAN. The problem is that it's outrageous. I had an appointment with you for four-thirty and you took me after six . . .

DOCTOR. Well, surely, you must realize . . .

WOMAN. No, no, I realize nothing of the sort. What makes you think that your time is more valuable, that my time is less valuable than yours? If you made an appointment you should keep to it.

DOCTOR. (*Pause.*) Mrs. Rudin, look.

WOMAN. No, you look. I'm alright. I'm fine, but people out there, there are worried people out there. Sitting, who knows *how* long, and you keep them there, they're waiting on your pleasure.

(*Pause.*)

DOCTOR. It isn't for my *pleasure* . . .

WOMAN. Then what is it for then?

DOCTOR. Mrs. . . .

WOMAN. Eh . . . ? Now what are two hours of *my* time worth? To you, obviously nothing.

DOCTOR. There are economic exigencies.

WOMAN. Are there?

DOCTOR. Yes, there are.

WOMAN. And what are they? (*Pause.*) What are they? That you think entitles you to treat people like cattle and then charge them like that?

DOCTOR. Mrs. Rudin, I am on call at three hospitals in New York, I maintain a complete . . .

WOMAN. That's your privilege. I didn't force you to do that. Those are *your* necessities. *Your* fiscal . . . *I* don't know. Why should I have to pay for that? (*Pause.*)

DOCTOR. Mrs. Rudin, what is your, now what is your complaint here?

WOMAN. I will not pay this bill. (*Pause.*)

DOCTOR. You won't.

WOMAN. I come here with a broken toe, I sit over three hours, and you take an x-ray and tell me my toe is broken. And you charge me for the x-ray and seventy-five dollars. (*Pause.*) I'm not going to pay it. (*Pause.*)

DOCTOR. These are my charges, for an office visit. For the first visit.

WOMAN. Well, you can find someone who will pay them, then, because I am not going to. (*Pause.*)

DOCTOR. There is a, there's a *contract* here.

WOMAN. There is, and what is that?

DOCTOR. You have taken my services; look, I don't like to talk about this.

WOMAN. I can see why you don't. Look me in the eye, there is a *contract* here? I have defrauded you of *services*? You charge me forty dollars for an x-ray and seventy-five dollars to tell me that my *toe is* broken, and you keep me waiting for three hours. You're goddamned *right* that you don't like to talk about it, 'cause you know that you are *wrong*. You *know* you're wrong.

DOCTOR. Well, you'll just have to take that question up with my accountants.

WOMAN. Fine. With your collection agency. Fine. I'll talk to them. I'll see you in small claims court. I don't care. This is not right. You call yourself a doctor. What you are is a thief. *You* live with yourself. No, I'm sorry. Prices what they are, *you* go out and work for a living. *You* go out there and support your family through what you do, and then tell me I should pay that to you. *You* do that. It's *nothing* to you. Nothing, to make people small. To deal with people who are frightened, who are hurt, I don't know, maybe who might think they're dying, and to keep them there *because* they're frightened, and then rob them. Go to hell, you can just go to hell. I damn you. Do you hear me? With your medical car license plates, and tell me there are exigencies? You can go to hell. I'll die before I'll pay that bill. I swear before God. Do you hear me?

DOCTOR. There's a distinct possibility . . .

WOMAN. You kiss my ass!

THE HAT

CUSTOMER. What do you think?
SALESWOMAN. You look wonderful. (*Pause.*)
CUSTOMER. Do you think so?
SALESWOMAN. I do.
CUSTOMER. With the veil?
SALESWOMAN. I don't know. Let's see. Let's try it on.
CUSTOMER. With this coat, though.
SALESWOMAN. Yes. Absolutely. (*Pause.*)
CUSTOMER. I'm going out tomorrow on this *interview?*
SALESWOMAN. Uh huh.
CUSTOMER. No. I don't like the veil. This hat, though, with this coat. (*Saleswoman nods.*) Yes.
SALESWOMAN. I think that's the nicest coat this season.
CUSTOMER. Do you think so?
SALESWOMAN. Far and away. Far and away.
CUSTOMER. Alright. I need the hat. This hat, this coat. (*Pause.*) This bag? (*Pause.*)
SALESWOMAN. For an interview?
CUSTOMER. Yes.
SALESWOMAN. I'm going to say "no."
CUSTOMER. No. I knew you would say that. No. You're right. Alright. The hat, the coat . . . oh, this is going to cost me, I know . . . not these boots, though?
SALESWOMAN. No.
CUSTOMER. Too casual.
SALESWOMAN. Yes.
CUSTOMER. Alright. Boots. Something dark. Black.
SALESWOMAN. . . . You have those ankle boots . . . ?
CUSTOMER. No, no, I want real boots. Dark. Long.
SALESWOMAN. Severe.
CUSTOMER. Very severe . . . alright. I need the boots. (*Pause.*) Pants?
SALESWOMAN. Or a skirt.

CUSTOMER. I thought pants. Something in dark green. You know? (*Pause.*)

SALESWOMAN. Well, you would have to be careful.

CUSTOMER. I know, I know. No, I know I would. And I thought a shawl-neck sweater. Something soft.

SALESWOMAN. Un huh.

CUSTOMER. In white. (*Pause.*) In off-white. In eggshell.

SALESWOMAN. Good. Sure.

CUSTOMER. This is going to cost me. But I *want* . . . do you know?

SALESWOMAN. Yes.

CUSTOMER. I *want*. When I walk *in* there . . .

SALESWOMAN. Yes.

CUSTOMER. I *want*. (*Pause.*) What do you think? Pants?

SALESWOMAN. Well, if you feel comfortable . . .

CUSTOMER. I would, I would. You know why? 'Cause it says something.

SALESWOMAN. Uh huh.

CUSTOMER. And it holds me in. It makes me stand up. I saw the ones that I want.

SALESWOMAN. Here?

CUSTOMER. Upstairs. Yes. A hundred-twenty dollars. (*Pause.*) What do you think on top?

SALESWOMAN. You've got the *sweater* . . .

CUSTOMER. Underneath.

SALESWOMAN. . . . Well . . .

CUSTOMER. Oh. oh! You know what? I saw it last month. You know, you know, underthings, an undergarment. (*Pause.*) One piece, you know, like a camisole.

SALESWOMAN. A teddy.

CUSTOMER. Yes. Yes. Just a little lace.

SALESWOMAN. That would be nice.

CUSTOMER. Silk. (*Pause.*) A teddy. Just a little *off*. A little *flush*, what do they call it, beige . . .

SALESWOMAN. Uh huh.

CUSTOMER. Not really beige. A little blusher. (*Smiles.*) I put a little blusher underneath. (*Pause.*) Just beneath the lace. Mmm? (*Saleswoman nods.*)

CUSTOMER. Alright. The slacks, the teddy, not the bag, the boots, the sweater. (*Pause.*) This is going to cost five hundred dollars.

SALESWOMAN. No.

CUSTOMER. Yes. With a new bag. Yes. (*Pause.*) But it's worth it, right? If I know when I walk in there?

SALESWOMAN. Yes.

CUSTOMER. Look! Look! Oh, look, look what she's got. The clutch bag. Yes. That bag. Yes. Do you think? With this coat.

SALESWOMAN. Yes.

CUSTOMER. 'Cause, 'cause, you know why? You've *got* it. Under *here.* (*Clutches imaginary bag under her arm.*) You know? So when you walk in there . . . you know? Just . . . just a small . . . just . . . just the perfect . . . you know? (*Pause.*) I have to have that bag. (*Pause. Shrugs.*) Yes, that bag. The slacks, the teddy, sweater . . . I couldn't get by with these boots, huh?

SALESWOMAN. No.

CUSTOMER. I know. They're great, though.

SALESWOMAN. Yes. They are.

CUSTOMER. (*Sighs.*) That bag's got to be two hundred dollars. (*Pause.*) How much is the hat?

SALESWOMAN. With or without the veil? (*Pause.*)

CUSTOMER. Without.

SALESWOMAN. Fifty-eight dollars.

CUSTOMER. And you're sure that you like it.

SALESWOMAN. You look lovely in it.

CUSTOMER. With this coat.

SALESWOMAN. With that coat. Absolutely.

CUSTOMER. (*Pause.*) I think so. (*Pause.*) I'll take it. Thank you. Thank you. You've been very . . .

SALESWOMAN. Not at all.

CUSTOMER. No, no. You have. You have been very gracious.

SALESWOMAN. Not at all.

CUSTOMER. Because I want to look nice for tomorrow.

SALESWOMAN. Well, you will.

CUSTOMER. (*Nods.*) Yes. Thank you. (*To self.*) With this hat.

SALESWOMAN. Anything else?

CUSTOMER. No.

BUSINESSMEN

(On an airplane.)

GREY. . . . Yes yes. We *had* eaten there!
BLACK. How did you find it?
GREY. Well . . .
BLACK. What did you have?
GREY. We had the fish.
BLACK. We never had the fish.
GREY. It wasn't good. (*Pause.*)
BLACK. No?
GREY. No. Not at all.
BLACK. We never had the fish.
GREY. It was not good.
BLACK. No?
GREY. No. (*Pause.*) It could have been that *night.*
BLACK. Uh huh.
GREY. I don't know. (*Pause.*)
BLACK. Well, we always enjoyed it greatly.
GREY. I'm sure. I am sure. No. (*Pause.*) The atmosphere was *fine.* The *wine*, the *wine* was good . . .
BLACK. Uh huh . . .
GREY. The *service* . . .
BLACK. Uh huh.
GREY. No. (*Pause.*) No, we should go back again.
BLACK. You should.
GREY. No. I think that we should.
BLACK. It probably was that night.
GREY. Yes. (*Pause.*) It very, very well could *have* been. (*Pause.*)
BLACK. What was it?
GREY. Sole.
BLACK. Mm. With sauce?
GREY. Yes. With some white wine sauce.
BLACK. Uh huh . . .
GREY. *You* know, with a . . . *yellow* sauce.

15

BLACK. Uh huh.

GREY. No, I'm sure that it was the fish. (*Nods.*) Fresh fish . . . (*Shakes head.*) You never know. (*Pause.*) No. When I was in the Army we had one whole company down sick one week.

BLACK. From fish?

GREY. Uh huh.

BLACK. Yes?

GREY. Fish soup.

BLACK. Uh huh. I don't doubt it.

GREY. Sick as dogs.

BLACK. Where was this?

GREY. Fort Sheridan.

BLACK. Uh huh.

GREY. Outside Chicago.

BLACK. Uh huh. (*Pause.*)

GREY. Sick as dogs.(*Pause.*)

BLACK. And this was your company?

GREY. No. No, thank God.

BLACK. Uh huh. (*Pause.*)

GREY. No. Got out of that one. (*Pause.*)

BLACK. Mmm. (*Pause.*)

GREY. I missed that one somehow.

BLACK. Uh huh.

GREY. I think that that's about the only *one* I missed.

BLACK. Uh huh.

GREY. You in the Army?

BLACK. No.

GREY. Armed services?

BLACK. No. (*Pause.*)

GREY. Uh huh. Uh huh. (*Pause.*) Yep. (*Pause.*) Used to go down into *Chicago* weekends.

BLACK. Uh huh.

GREY. Raise all *kind* of hell down there.

BLACK. Down in Chicago.

GREY. Well, yeah. The base is just about an hour bus ride from *town*, eh? Fort *Sheridan*.

BLACK. Uh huh.

GREY. (*Meditatively.*) Yep. (*Pause.*) There used to be this *chili* parlor on the, just across, just kitty-corner from the bus, on, on the *corner* . . . the *corner* . . . of Clark and Lake Streets. Underneath the Elevated. (*Pause.*)

16

BLACK. Uh huh.

GREY. *Good* chili. (*Pause.*) Good chili. (*Pause.*) Good coffee. (*Pause.*) My *God* that tasted good, out in the cold. (*Pause.*) In those cold winters. (*Pause.*) I can still taste it. We would sit, we would sit in the window, steamy. Smoking *cigarettes.* (*Pause.*) Looking out the window. Underneath the El . . . (*Pause.*) Steamy . . . (*Pause.*) Well, I'd better get some *work* done here. (*Takes out pad and pencil.*)

BLACK. Yes, I best had, too.

GREY. You going home?

BLACK. No, going to work. (*Pause.*) You?

GREY. Going home.

BLACK. Good for you.

COLD

(A man, "A," waiting for a subway, another man, "B," comes down into the subway and looks up and down the track.)

A. Everybody always looks both ways. Although they always know which way the train is coming from. Did you ever notice that?

B. Yes. I did. *(Pause.)*

A. You going home?

B. Yes. *(Pause.)*

A. I'm going home, too . . . Did you ever notice sometimes when it's cold you feel *wet?* *(Pause.)*

B. Yes. *(Pause. A looks up.)*

A. *(Of grating overhead.)* They make those things to let in *air.* *(Pause.)*

B. Uh huh.

A. From outside. Listen: Listen . . . *(Pause.)* Where are you going now?

B. Home.

A. Do you live near here?

B. No.

A. Where do you live? *(Pause.)*

B. Downtown.

A. Where?

B. Downtown.

A. Where, though? *(Pause.)*

B. In Soho.

A. Is it nice there?

B. Yes.

A. *(Pause.)* Is it warm?

B. Yes. *(Pause.)* Sometimes it's not so warm.

A. When wind gets in, right? When the wind gets in?

B. Right.

A. So what do you do then? *(Pause.)* What do you do then?

B. You . . . stop it up.

19

A. Uh huh. (*Pause.*)
B. *Or* . . . you can put covers on the windows.
A. Covers.
B. Yes. Storm covers. (*Pause.*)
A. Storm covers.
B. To keep out the draft.
A. And does that keep the draft out?
B. Yes.
A. Have you been waiting long?
B. No. (*Pause.*)
A. *How* long? (*Pause.*)
B. Several minutes. (*Pause.*)
A. Are you going home now?
B. Yes. (*Looks at sound of subway in the distance.*)
A. That's the other track. (*They watch the train passing.*) Do you live alone?
B. No. (*Pause.*)
A. You live with someone?
B. Yes.
A. Are you happy? (*Pause.*)
B. Yes.
A. Are they there now?
B. (*Pause.*) I think so. (*Pause.*)
A. What are they called?
B. Hey, look, what business is it of yours what they're called. (*Pause.*) You understand? (*Pause.*)

EPILOGUE

MAN. I love the way the sun goes down. One moment it is dark, the next, light.

PROPERTY PLOT

DOCTOR
  Bill (Woman)
THE HAT
  Hat with veil (Customer)
  Coat (Customer)
  Handbag (Customer)
  Boots (Customer)
BUSINESSMEN
  Pad and Pencil (Grey)

PRAIRIE DU CHIEN

PRAIRIE DU CHIEN was first produced by "Earplay" for National Public Radio in April, 1979. The director was Daniel Freudenberger; and the cast was Charles Durning, Jeff Goldblum, Larry Block and Bruno Kirby.

SCENE

The play takes place in a railroad parlor car heading west through Wisconsin in 1910. The time is three a.m.

CHARACTERS

A PORTER

A CARD DEALER

A GIN PLAYER

A STORYTELLER

A LISTENER

THE LISTENER'S SON

Note: Directions in brackets pertain to radio production.

PRAIRIE DU CHIEN

[*Sound: The continuous lulling
sound of a railroad journey. We listen a while.*]

(*Note: All voices, except where indicated, should be very subdued, as
suited to three a.m.*)

[*Sound: Cards being shuffled.
Sound: Train whistling approach-
ing a crossing. Long. Long. Short.
Long.*]

DEALER. Cut.
GIN PLAYER. I pass the cut.
DEALER. Right.

[*Sound: Cards being dealt.*]

One, one, Two, Two. Three and Three.

[*Sound: Dealer yawns.*]

GIN PLAYER. You tired?
DEALER. No. And four and four. Five *five*, six *six*, and Seven
seven, eight, *eight*, nine and *ten*.
GIN PLAYER. Good.
DEALER. Three of diamonds. (*Yawns.*) He takes the three of
diamonds.

[*Sound: Porter approaching.*]

(*Pause.*) And throws the king. (*Pause.*) Throws the cowboy.
PORTER. Yassuh. Anything else I can get you gentlemen?
DEALER. No. Thank you.
GIN PLAYER. No.

[*Sound: Money jingling.*]

DEALER. Here.
PORTER. Thank you very *much* sir.
DEALER. Sure. Throws the K.

[*Sound: Porter retreating.*]

GIN PLAYER. Play.
DEALER. Yah. (*Pause.*) I play the king right back. (*Pause.*)
And I get the *heart* five. (*Pause.*) The five of hearts. What does

25

that tell us? (*Pause.*) When he has taken the three diamonds? (*Pause.*) When he has took the three of dimes?

> [*Sound: The door to the car opens. Rushes of air, etc. The door is closed. Sound: We follow the footsteps of the person who has just come in. As he walks down the aisle the conversation of the card players fades.*]

GIN PLAYER. It's your play.
DEALER. Yes. Alright. You use that? (*Pause.*) Eh? That's what I thought. And plays the ten.

> [*Sound: The footsteps stop.*]

STORYTELLER. (*Expels air.*) Cold out there! (*In an undertone.*)
LISTENER. I'll bet it is.
STORYTELLER. Phew! The boy still asleep?
LISTENER. Yep.
STORYTELLER. I wish I could sleep like that.
DEALER. (*In the background.*) Jack.
STORYTELLER. 'Specially on a *long* ride.
LISTENER. Yes.
STORYTELLER. A *night* train. (*Pause.*) Never *could* sleep. (*Pause.*) *Never* sleep. Where was I?
DEALER. Take it.
LISTENER. Up in Council Bluffs, I think.
STORYTELLER. That's right. Now I was *telling* you I'm up in Council Bluffs.
DEALER. The six of diamonds. Six of diamonds and the five of hearts. Go on and take it. Take it, 'cause you *know* you want it.
GIN PLAYER. Well, I don't know if I want it yet, or not.
STORYTELLER. . . . And this man owned a *drygoods* store. I'd see him five, six times a year when I'd swing through. Eh? Always good for a small order. Nothing great. But steady.
LISTENER. Right.
STORYTELLER. He had a lovely little wife.
LISTENER. A young man.
STORYTELLER. In his fifties.
LISTENER. Uh huh.
STORYTELLER. In his fifties. (*Pause.*) And married two years at the time, perhaps. At that time that I speak of. (*Pause.*) He had a small farm out of town.

26

LISTENER. Yes.

STORYTELLER. (*Pause.*) He might have *been* something back east. But I don't know exactly. No one knew. Not even afterwards.

DEALER. Four.

GIN PLAYER. You're going down with four?

DEALER. Yes. Yes. I think I am.

STORYTELLER. And his wife?

LISTENER. Yes?

STORYTELLER. My *God* she was a pretty thing.

LISTENER. Mmm.

STORYTELLER. And he was a jealous man. A very jealous man. Of money, too. Very tight-fisted. Always thought that he was being cheated. I can tell you. Smart, though. (*Pause.*) A clever man. (*Pause.*) There was talk he'd been a lawyer in the east.

LISTENER. Mmm.

STORYTELLER. And he was always bitter. As if he'd come *down*, you know? (*Pause.*) As if he'd come *down*, in life. (*Pause.*) Very bitter. *She* was kind, though. (*Pause.*) To me. A lovely woman. (*Pause.*) When I'd come through. If she was in the store. They lived out on the farm. I told you?

LISTENER. Yes.

STORYTELLER. Just out of town. Him and their hand and her. (*Pause.*) And she was just not happy. When I saw her. As the months went by. I saw her fade. (*Pause.*)

> [*Sound: The slap of cards.*]

(*The Storyteller sighs.*) And then one time when I came in. (*Pause.*) And this is what I told you. (*Pause.*) I saw the welts.

> [*Sound: From the back of the car we hear low whistling: "The Banks Of The Wabash."*]*

(*Pause.*) I saw bruises on her face and hands.

LISTENER. Mmm.

STORYTELLER. I had just come in. One day in March. She came up to the store. She had been driven by their hand. This colored man. He stayed down in the wagon and she came inside.

LISTENER. When was this?

*See special note on copyright page.

27

STORYTELLER. Spring. March. Sometimes warm. Disturbing. Wet. One day cold, this one warm. I could see she was disturbed. She drew him in the corner. They had you know, they had words. He turned to me: "What are you looking at?" he says. And there was *hate* in his eyes . . . ?
LISTENER. Mmm.
STORYTELLER. I mean to tell you. (*Pause.*) And then he took to ask me when I'd come in, had I seen his *wife*. (*Pause.*) Had I seen her on the street . . . in any other town . . . He said: "I worry when I'm not at home," his eyes, he had this tone, sarcastic, and you never knew if he was serious or what. (*Pause. Mimicking.*) "Have you seen my *wife*?" In town they told me he would check the buggy horses in the evening when he got home to see were they *tired*. (*Pause.*) If they'd been *out*.
LISTENER. Why didn't he ask the hired man?
STORYTELLER. He didn't trust him. Not by this time. Not at all.
DEALER. (*Faintly.*) You know you want it.
STORYTELLER. No. (*Pause.*) He was sure that she was stepping out on him. He had seen, he said that he had seen . . . (Sotto.) Is the boy asleep?
LISTENER. Yes.
STORYTELLER. *Traces* . . . (*Pause.*) Eh?
LISTENER. Yes.
STORYTELLER. And he knew that she had been unfaithful. (*Pause.*)
DEALER. You know you want it. Soo-cide jacks, Man with the Axe. Go on and take it.
STORYTELLER. He knew she was stepping out. I'll tell you: one day my route brought me back. When I was swinging back I come in to the store. He has a *grin* on his face? (*Pause.*) Such a strange grin.
LISTENER. Mmm.
STORYTELLER. Not healthy. Not at all. In August. (*Pause.*) Dust in the air. (*Pause.*) Murder in the air. (*Pause.*) You could feel it. Animals could feel it. (*Pause.*) I tried to pass the time of day with him. He couldn't hear a word I said. "What is it, friend?" I said. "What's on your mind?" "I'm going to kill my wife," he says.
DEALER. He takes the four.

28

STORYTELLER. "I'll tell you," he says. "If you ask. She's going to have a child. It isn't mine. And I am going to kill her." (*Pause.*) "She's going to tell me who the father is, and then I'll kill her." Well. (*Pause.*) I tried talking to the man. I tried to keep him there. But he would not be held. We struggled. I don't think it was a contest. He was full of strength from hate. He hit me with something. He knocked me down. (*Pause.*) When I got up he was gone. (*Pause.*) I went for the sheriff.

[*Sound: Whistling stops.*]

LISTENER. Were you hurt?

STORYTELLER. I was not hurt. No. No. I found the sheriff. And I told him. Just what I told *you.* We rode out to the farm. From on a crest, about a half a mile out we saw a glow. The farm was burning. In the dusk. The barn was burning. We rode to the house. What did we see? (*Pause.*) On the porch. The farmer. Hanging from the crossbeam. Dead. His shotgun on the ground.

LISTENER. He hung himself?

STORYTELLER. Wait. And we heard. What sounded like a woman crying. In the house. (*Pause.*) Softly crying. Softly. (*Pause.*) The sheriff went inside. (*Pause.*) Cautiously. I waited on the porch. (*Pause.*) I heard voices. (*Pause.*) I heard, it sounded like: "Go to the barn." A woman's voice. "Go to the barn. Please. Help him."

GIN PLAYER. Twelve.

DEALER. And three from twelve is nine.

STORYTELLER. So I went to the barn. (*Pause.*) Burning. Burning. Through the doorway I could see the hired man. (*Pause.*) He was dead. (*Pause.*) Lying in the middle of the barn. He had a harness in his hand, and he had had a pitchfork stuck right up beneath his heart. (*Pause.*) And he'd been cut. His overalls were ripped down and the man had cut him. (*Pause.*) It was sickening. Five feet away there was the woman. In this lovely dress. This red dress. On her face. Her back was blowed away. And both of 'em are dead. (*Pause.*) And the barn's about to go.

DEALER. You want it? Do you want the card?

GIN PLAYER. Yes.

STORYTELLER. And the barn's about to go. (*Pause.*) Well, I start back to the house. Eh? On the way I meet the sheriff coming down. He says, "Come on." "The nigger's in the barn." "I

29

know," I say. "He's dead." "You sure he's dead?" the sheriff says. "Yes," I say. "Yes. I'm sure. Her, too. The both of 'em are dead." "Who?" he says. "Both of who?" "Him and the wife. The hand and her. He's killed 'em both." "No. (*Pause.*) He says. "Don't tell me that she's dead. Don't tell me that she's dead when I just saw her in the house." "Saw who?" "The wife. Mrs. McGurney," he says, "In the house. She told me to come down here. (*Pause.*) She told me to look in the barn." "Well, someone's dead," I say. "Him and a woman. Some white woman." We run to the barn. And he is talking to himself. He's mumbling, "She told me to come *down* here. No. To help the nigger." (*Pause.*) We get there, barn's about to go now, any second. Cinders in the air as big as your hand. We stood in the door. The sheriff shouts "Hallo!" The smoke blows. There they are. The two of them. (*Pause.*) In the middle of the barn. He's on his back. And she, I don't know, she has *crawled* to him. I would have sworn that she was dead. (*Pause.*) She has *moved* to him, and she has got her head upon his chest. "That's her!" he says. "That's her!" "That's *who?*" (*Pause.*) I said. "Who?" And then the barn caved in.

GIN PLAYER. Porter!

[*Sound: Porter approaches.*]

PORTER. Yassuh?

GIN PLAYER. What time is it?

PORTER. Two fifty-three, sir.

GIN PLAYER. Thank you.

[*Sound: Porter retreats.*]

STORYTELLER. "That's who?" I said. "Mrs. McGurney."

DEALER. Okay, then. That's sixty that you owe me, sixty, sixty-two, we'll call it sixty.

GIN PLAYER. Thank you.

[*Sound: Humming "Redwing."*]*

STORYTELLER. "Now wait," I say. "Wait. Didn't you just say you saw her in the *house?*" (*Pause.*) There was something in the air then. (*Pause.*) As if the air got thick. The barn was so hot. We fell back. The sheriff's shaking. He started to walk. To go back to the house. There was a smell like, I don't know. Like sweat. Like sick sweat. Do you know? We went back. (*Pause.*) And we went in. And all the time he mumbled to himself. "No.

*See special note on copyright page.

No." (*Pause.*) Very softly. We went in. And room by room we searched the house. We started in the cellar. There was no one there. (*Pause.*) There was no one there. In the whole house. (*Pause.*) We searched every room. Up to the attic. (*Listener makes a shivering sound.*) He'd seen her. (*Pause.*) He said he'd seen her. I heard something. (*Pause.*) And I would swear to that. But he said that he'd seen the woman. There was nothing in the house. Until as we were coming down the attic stairs. "Look. Look!" he said. Then I saw something. To this day I could not tell you what it was. A form. (*Pause.*) Something blowing. I don't know. "It's *her*!" he says. It went into the bedroom. Something went. I don't know. (*Pause.*) The door slammed. (*Pause.*)

DEALER. You deal.

GIN PLAYER. *High* card deals.

DEALER. I'm sorry. You are absolutely right.

> [*Sound: Porter enunciates first line of chorus softly: "Now the Moon shines tonight on Little Redwing . . ." continues humming.*]

STORYTELLER. We went in. Through the bedroom door. (*Pause.*) We opened the bedroom door. (*Pause.*) There was no one in the room. The window was down and locked. (*Pause.*) There was only one door in the room besides the one we came in through. And it went to the closet.

DEALER. Nine and nine and ten and ten and three of diamonds.

STORYTELLER. And we stood there. (*Pause.*) He cocked his gun. (*Pause.*) And he motioned me to stand to one side. (*Pause.*) Well, my friend, I began to pray.

GIN PLAYER. Five.

STORYTELLER. He moved to pull the closet door back. Then the door *behind* us was flung open. Well, we spun around. There were these three men from the town. (*Pause.*) Gaping at us. "Get out!" they said. "Get out cause she's coming down!" The house had caught a cinder from the barn "Get out!" they said. "She's burning!" "No, I'm *coming* out," he says. "I'm *coming* out. I'm checking." "Well, you *best* get out," they said. And they went. We could hear them going through the house. "Haloooo! Is anybody there?" (*Pause.*) "Is anybody here?" He locked the door. He locked us in the room. He looked at me, and then he locked us in the room. And he stared at the closet. I heard

31

something. I think that I heard something. It could have been the wind. (*Pause.*) It could be crying. Softly crying. In the closet. (*Pause.*) He grasped the handle, and he threw it open. There was no one there. (*Pause.*) It was empty. Except for this dress. This pretty red dress. (*Pause.*) And it was burning. (*Pause.*) The hem was burning. All around. As if that it had just been lit. The flames were rising. "For the love of God, let's leave here," I said. "Please." "Oh *no!*" (*Pause.*) He was moaning to himself. "No!" The room was full of smoke. I had to drag him from the closet, door. "Come on, man. For God's *sake* come on . . . !" (*Pause.*) I met the townsmen on the stairs. "You have to help me," I said. "He's had too much smoke." We dragged him from the house. The house was burning down, the barn was gone. (*Pause.*) The two bodies still inside. We watched the rafters fall. The night was gray. It was a strange, gray color, and the air was full of smells. We left the sheriff by the house. When we came back he was asleep. We woke him up. We all were going back to town. (*Pause.*) There was going to be an autopsy.

LISTENER. On the storekeeper.

STORYTELLER. On him, yes. He was the only one. We all gave depositions at the courthouse. This is what he said. "I have been sleeping." This is what the sheriff said. "I have been sleeping. We rode out there. He was hanging. They were dead inside the barn." And then he went to sleep. (*Pause.*) In the courthouse. (*Pause.*) He could not stay awake.

DEALER. Twelve.

GIN PLAYER. And twenty's thirty-two.

STORYTELLER. He could not stay awake. And they thought he was ill. But there was nothing wrong with him.

GIN PLAYER. Deal.

STORYTELLER. Three years later he was killed.

LISTENER. The sheriff.

STORYTELLER. From the night the barn burned he was never right. They told me. When I came through. (*Pause.*) *Never* right. He slept the whole time. (*Pause.*) His wife deserted him. (*Pause.*) He lost his job, of course.

LISTENER. Yes.

STORYTELLER. He was not well. (*Pause.*) And then this man caught him. There had been *stories* . . . Is the boy asleep?

LISTENER. Yes. (*Pause.*)

STORYTELLER. There had (*whispering*) been these *stories* . . . and then this man caught him with his daughter.
LISTENER. Caught the sheriff with his daughter.
STORYTELLER. Yuh.
LISTENER. How old was she? (*Pause.*)
STORYTELLER. Ten. (*Pause.*) Ten years old.
LISTENER. No!

> [*Sound: Train approaches crossing and whistle hoots. Long, long short long.*]

STORYTELLER. Yes. He told him, listen to this: "I am going to take my daughter home. You tell me where you're going to be. Because I have to talk to you." The sheriff told him he would be at home. (*Pause.*) Eh?
LISTENER. Yes.
STORYTELLER. Ten years old. (*Pause.*) And the man went to his house. He went in. He called. This is what I'm told. (*Pause.*) There was no one there. (*Pause.*) He heard someone rocking. On the floor above. (*Pause.*) Rocking in a chair. He heard the squeaking. He went up. He threw the door back and there was the sheriff. In a rocking chair.
DEALER. He takes the jack, he doesn't take the ten.
STORYTELLER. There is the sheriff dressed in a red dress. (*Pause.*) A red gingham dress. (*Pause.*) Rocking. (*Pause.*) He said, "Please help him. They are in the barn. (*Pause.*) Help him. Please." (*Pause.*)
DEALER. Eight.
STORYTELLER. "Please help him."
DEALER. Eight.
GIN PLAYER. You call with *eight*? The hell you say! (*Pause.*) Lay them down. Just lay them down and let's see what you've got.
STORYTELLER. In a red gingham dress. (*Pause.*) "Help him. Help him. Please."
DEALER. Here, count 'em up yourself.
GIN PLAYER. I will, yes thank you.
DEALER. Have you had enough?
GIN PLAYER. What? No.
STORYTELLER. Dressed like a lady. Eh? And rocking back and forth.
LISTENER. What happened to the animals?

33

GIN PLAYER. Cut for the deal.
STORYTELLER. What animals?
DEALER. Six.
GIN PLAYER. Four.
DEALER. Six deals.
LISTENER. The *animals*. (*Pause.*) In the barn.
STORYTELLER. *McGurney's* barn.
LISTENER. Yes.
STORYTELLER. What about them? You mean when the *barn* burned.
LISTENER. Yes. (*Pause.*)
STORYTELLER. What about them.
LISTENER. Were they in the barn.
DEALER. Six *six*, and seven *seven*, eight and eight . . .
STORYTELLER. Yes.
DEALER. Nine and ten and king of clubs.
LISTENER. Why didn't they die? (*Pause.*)
STORYTELLER. Well, I guess they *did*. (*Pause.*) I guess that they *did*. (*Pause.*) I guess that they *did*.
DEALER. He takes the three of clubs.
STORYTELLER. The horses and the cows . . .
GIN PLAYER. May I please see your cards?
STORYTELLER. (*To himself.*) All dead . . .
DEALER. I'm sorry . . . ?
GIN PLAYER. May I see your cards?
DEALER. You want to see my cards.
GIN PLAYER. Yes.
STORYTELLER. (*To himself.*) Yep, yep, yep, yep, yep.
DEALER. Why do you want to see my cards?
GIN PLAYER. Just put 'em down.

> [*Sound: Way back in the car the Porter has started humming to himself "Meet Me In St. Louis."*]*

DEALER. I . . . wait. I want to tell you something.
GIN PLAYER. Lay your cards down.
DEALER. I've got ten cards in my hand, friend. Same as you.
GIN PLAYER. I'm asking nicely. (*Pause.*) I want to see your hand.

*See special note on copyright page.

DEALER. And what if I don't want to show it to you? (*Pause.*)
I'm not cheating you, friend. (*Pause.*) I'm not cheating you.
GIN PLAYER. (*Raising his voice.*) Count out your cards. Just
lay 'em down and count 'em.
DEALER. (*Pause.*) Alright. One. Two. Three. Four, five, six.
(*Pause.*) Seven. (*Pause.*) Eight. (*Pause.*) Nine, ten. Eh? Are you
satisfied. You owe me eighty-seven dollars. (*Pause.*) It's time to
settle up.
GIN PLAYER. I want to play some more.
DEALER. You do?
GIN PLAYER. (*Pause.*) Yes.
DEALER. (*Pause.*) Alright.
STORYTELLER. So where you folks coming from?
LISTENER. Chicago.
STORYTELLER. Mmm. (*Pause.*) Where you going to?
LISTENER. Duluth.
STORYTELLER. The boy in school?
LISTENER. Yes.
STORYTELLER. Mmm. (*Pause.*) Fine-looking boy.
DEALER. Cut for the deal.
STORYTELLER. Up to Duluth, eh?
LISTENER. Yes.
GIN PLAYER. Five.
DEALER. A doctor. King of hearts. I deal.

> [*Sound: Sound of train changes
> slightly.*]

PORTER. (*To himself.*) We coming down the hill for water.
Five minutes we be crost the bridge. I always tell it by the soun'.
DEALER. And two and two and three and three. (*Pause.*) Four,
four, five, five, the six and six and seven, seven, eight, eight,
nine and ten. (*Pause.*) Two of spades.
GIN PLAYER. Pass.
DEALER. I pass, too.
STORYTELLER. (*To himself.*) The skirt in flames around her
ankles.
DEALER. Two.
GIN PLAYER. Two. I take it.
STORYTELLER. . . . From the hem.
DEALER. Three.
STORYTELLER. . . . Lapping up. As if that it had just been
lighted.

35

DEALER. Four. He drops the three, he drops the four.
GIN PLAYER. Just play.
STORYTELLER. And sleeping with the hired man.
DEALER. A stranger. Queen of clubs.
STORYTELLER. . . . The boy asleep?
DEALER. The queen of clubs.
LISTENER. Yes . . .
STORYTELLER. Heavy with his child. (*Pause.*) They say.
DEALER. Takes the queen.
STORYTELLER. You can't know. Many things. You travel on a route up here.
DEALER. He takes it.
STORYTELLER. (*To himself.*) *Many* things.
DEALER. He takes the queen and throws the ten.
STORYTELLER. They think that they can talk to you, 'cause they see you so seldom.
PORTER. (*To himself.*) Slowin' down.
GIN PLAYER. (*Yelling.*) You son of a bitch! You're crimping *cards* on me! Don't touch that hand!
DEALER. Now, wait. Now look: Look, we'll just throw it in. Just pay me what you owe me and let's quit. Alright. Look, we'll just throw it in . . .
GIN PLAYER. Don't you touch those cards you . . .

[*Sound: A pistol fired twice.*]

PORTER. Oh, my sweet Jesus!
BOY. Poppa!
LISTENER. (*Sotto.*) Don't move. (*Pause.*)
GIN PLAYER. Did I hit you?
DEALER. Oh, my God . . .
STORYTELLER. Whyn't you give me that gun, mister. Whyn't you just hand it to me . . . ?
GIN PLAYER. Did I hit you? (*Pause.*)
STORYTELLER. Why don't you give me the gun?
GIN PLAYER. Did I hit you?
DEALER. No.
STORYTELLER. Give me the gun. That's good. Give me the gun. Good. (*Pause.*)
LISTENER. Did he hit the man?
STORYTELLER. No. Now you sit down. Just sit down. Good, now.
BOY. Poppa . . . ?

36

LISTENER. It's alright.

BOY. What happened?

LISTENER. Nothing. These men had a fight. (*Pause.*) It's alright. Go back to sleep. (*Pause.*) Everything's alright now.

BOY. Where are we?

LISTENER. You go to sleep. We have a long long time to go yet.

GIN PLAYER. He. (*Pause.*) He was cheating me.

DEALER. No one was cheating you. You're *crazy*, friend. (*Pause.*) Eh? You're *crazy*, fellow.

GIN PLAYER. He was crimping cards.

DEALER. Where? Where? Show me one card. Show me one card marked. (*Pause.*) Eh? You son of a bitch. They ought to lock you up. They ought to take a *strap* to you. (*Pause.*) If you can't lose, don't *play*.

GIN PLAYER. (*Pause.*) I'm sorry.

DEALER. Well, you owe me eighty-seven dollars here. (*Pause.*)

GIN PLAYER. Yes. Yes.

> [*Sound: Train whistles. Sound: Train begins to slow down.*]

Here. Yes. Thank you.

> [*Sound: Porter walking through car.*]

PORTER. Water stop. This. Prairie du Chien. Just about five minutes. Anybody want to stretch they legs we taking on some water.

> [*Sound: Train whistle.*]

GIN PLAYER. Eighty. Eighty-five. Six. Seven.

> [*Sound: Train coming to a stop. Blowing off of steam.*]

I'm sorry.

PORTER. Prairie du Chien.

DEALER. Get me my bag, eh?

PORTER. Yassuh.

> [*Sound: Bag being taken from rack. Panting. Sound: Progress of Porter and Dealer walking through car with bags.*]

PORTER. I got it, you just watch your step, suh, getting down. (*Pause. We listen to the sounds of the train taking on water, cooling, etc.*)

STORYTELLER. Well! (*Pause.*) Well, I think that I'll step down and get some air. (*Pause.*) Join me?

LISTENER. (*Softly.*) Son? (*Pause.*) Son? (*Pause.*)

STORYTELLER. Is that boy asleep again?

LISTENER. Son?

STORYTELLER. Can you beat that? (*Pause.*) I'd give a lot to sleep like that. (*Pause.*) Yes, I would. Yessir, I would.

> [*Sound: We listen to the sound of the train for a moment.*]

PROPERTY PLOT

Deck of playing cards (Dealer)

Coins (Dealer and Gin Player)

Pistol (Gin Player)

Luggage (Porter)

A Sermon

A SERMON was written as a companion piece for a 1979 Chicago revival of *Sexual Perversity in Chicago*. It featured Cosmo White and, later, W.H. Macy, and was directed by Sheldon Patinkin.

CHARACTER

CLERGYMAN

A Sermon

In September, 1939 a dentist in Viceroy, Louisiana placed a human tooth into a jar of Coca Cola and let it stand overnight. The next morning Hitler invaded Poland. A man has a deaf yak. The yak cannot hear. It grew up deaf. And this man speaks to it: "How are you today, King?" "Bow wow," says the yak one day. Bow wow. And the next day the yak goes "moo." (*Pause.*) The animal has no *idea* of its responsabi*li*ties. It knows that something is required of it; it knows that it should make a *sound*, but it has no idea what that sound is supposed to be. Life is like that. I feel. If it were not one thing it would surely be another. It *is*, however, one thing. Though it is by no means the *same* thing. Although it's always something of that nature.

And kindness starts at home. You cannot beat your pets and come quick on your wife and pretend you forgot to take the garbage out and go be nice to whales. It's not *right*, it's trans*par*ent, and it makes you *look* bad, too.

Our most cherished illusions — what are they but hastily constructed cofferdams restraining homosexual panic.

Let's talk about love. (*Pause.*) Love. My golly, it sells diapers, don't it!

Love is the mucilage that sticks the tattered ribbons of experience — the stiff construction-paper indians and pumpkins of experience — to the scrapbook of our lives.

And there may be many *kinds* of love:

Love may be the Rocky Coast of Maine, with boats and saltspray gooshing up and you all cozy in the rented cabin.

All the others have gone down. Gone down to Boston, gone back to New York. His hands are pressing into the small of your back. His breath is hot upon your shoulder. You have come to write and he has forced the lock. You've never *seen* this man, he followed you home from the pier. But do you care? You care very much. You whack him with the cover of your typewriter. Whack, whack, whack. Whack, whack, whack. Whack, whack, whack. You hit him on the head. And he gets off, he pulls his

43

trousers up and leaves. (*Pause.*) You go back to work. You're typing. "September 18th. Today dawned bleak and sere and I was up to see it. Surely there must be an end to time . . . "

You look down to read back your sentence to yourself. What do you see but weak and colorless impressions. Your ribbon has run out. Oh well, that's a fair excuse to go up to the Lodge to share a cup of coffee with the Kind Old Woman who runs the resort.

You open the door. You breathe in the cold, life-giving spray. The Old Man from the Pier hits you on the head with an oar and he jumps on your bones. And this time he had brought his friends.

And what of Death? (*Pause.*) What *of* it? That's my question. All of us are going to die, but nobody believes it. And if we did believe it we would not go to the office. We would call in sick.

Everybody's talking about "Death." Nobody's been there. Yes, yes, yes, there is a rash of testimony to the effect that Ms So-and-So or Mr. Whossis once was dead for thirty-seconds, or something, and it was just like going through a car wash.

You lay back and it is warm and wet outside. But you feel nothing. Whiirrrr, whiirrrr, and here comes the soap. And everything clouds over. Then you hear a hum. And that must be the brushes. Everything goes white, then black, then white again. You feel a buffeting. There is a wall of water/ It cascades over the windshield, wetting all, and driving off the sludge, the salt, the road-dirt and the soap. Until you're clean. You're clean.

Then comes the hot wax. — analogous in the experience of death to — what? (*Pause.*) *Exactly*. Hot wax coursing for a mere half-dollar more with ten bucks worth of gas. (Well worth it) making your car shine. Shine on. Shine on, my car. (*Pause.*)

Five youths dressed in coveralls drop upon you like ministering angels, rub your imperfections out and then move on. You'd better *tip* them, though, cause you'll be back this way again! There you go. Out into traffic. And how *proud* you feel. And why not? (*Pause.*) this is death. You've been there *before*, you say . . . well, you're going there again.

And sickness. Is it real?

And suffering? (*Pause.*) Are they real? (*Pause.*)

Yesterday a man was going to the supermarket. There he went. Upon some errand. His head full of news or gossip. *Fiscal* problems . . . (They are never really far away . . .) He turned the corner and he trod upon the mat which would open the door, and he walked on. The door, however, some of you have already guessed, did not open. Not a jot. (*Pause.*) He slammed right into it and broke his nose.

His blood flowed. As many times may happen, attendant upon a sharper blow to that area—particularly such a blow to one unused to violent contact—he began to cry. (*Pause.*)

Many who had seen his accident were laughing at the picture that it made. And then we heard him cry. And then he turned, and then we saw the blood. (*Pause.*)

"I've broke my nose," he rather oinked. "I've broke my nose, and you all think it's funny. (*Pause.*) He could not think of what to say; a phrase which might instill in us, the spectators who deigned to ridicule his pain, shame or remorse. His mind searched for a curse. (*Pause.*) "Fuck you", he said. (*Pause.*) Fuck you.

What is required of us? To whom do we owe alleigance, and is this a laughing matter, or should we just mope around as if the dog died?

This is a good question, and, in conclusion let me say the following:

A traveller is in the desert. He has lost his way. He has no water. And he is near death. Far off he sees a mountain. In the distance. Far away. Ice encapsulates its top and flows in freshets down its sides, and becomes springs and rivers. Cool, fresh water, redolent of trout. Clean, unpolluted, there for all to drink, to bathe in, to enjoy. And he knows it is a mirage. (*Pause.*) There *is* no mountain there. There is but desert. But he trudges on toward it in any case. (*Pause.*) Whom should we identify with in this story? (*Pause.*) How many thought the trout? It's not the trout. It not the trout at all. We've *all* been down. We've all been at the end of our rope. We all know what it is to call on powers—and let's pray that they exits—far greater than ourselves; to call out, "Lord . . . Lord, this world of yours sucks *hippo* dick, I just can't hack it anymore. "And what answer was forthcoming? (*Pause.*) Exactly.

Therefore, let's smile. Let's slap a silly grin on our face that says to all the world, "Yes, I see what's going on, but I'm pretending not to notice. I see the misery . . . the pain . . . the hopes frustrated in our daily lives . . . the fear of lonliness . . .

the fear of death . . . " I'm going to skip to the end of this list . . . ". . . and through it all I *smile*, and I say, with the prophets: 'Lo, this world has been the same a great long while. It all shall be the same a hundred years from now—probably sooner.' " (*Pause.*)

And that's it.

Therefore be well. Peace to you. Be very kind to one another in your daily lives. And clean up when you're done.

Good evening, and Amen.

SHOESHINE

SHOESHINE was first produced at The Ensemble Studio Theatre in New York City. It was directed by W.H. Macy and featured the following cast: Everett Ensley; Arthur French; Pirie MacDonald; Joseph Jamroy; Colin Stinton; and Trey Hunt.

SCENE

Sam's Shoeshine Parlor. Afternoon.

CHARACTERS

SAM .... A middle-aged black man

JIM .... A young black man

MILLER ⎫
        ⎬ .... Two middle-aged white men
FOX ⎭

DOWD .... A white man

A CUSTOMER .... A white man

SHOESHINE

JIM. You want me to do these?

SAM. They got a shine ticket on it?

JIM. I *saw* it . . .

SAM. You did . . . ?

JIM. Yeah. It must of gone down in the boot.

SAM. No, no. I'm saying that is *has* a ticket on it.

JIM. I know that it has. I got it. Here it is. (*Pause.*) You want me to do 'em?

SAM. Yeah. You start on 'em.

JIM. Which ones here?

SAM. The *brown* there. Just like you're doing.

JIM. Alright. (*Pause.*)

SAM. And those ones there?

JIM. The red?

SAM. Yeah.

JIM. Uh huh . . .

SAM. When you get to them you tell me.

JIM. Alright.

SAM. 'Cause that bitch come in here yesterday . . .

JIM. Uh huh.

SAM. She said we fucked them up.

JIM. We didn't fuck them up.

SAM. I know we didn't. (*Pause.*)

JIM. She fucked 'em up her *own* self if she fucked 'em up.

SAM. I know she did. (*Pause.*)

JIM. Uh huh. (*Pause.*) You got a cigarette? (*Sam takes out his pack of cigarettes. Jim comes over and takes two.*) Thank you.

SAM. That's alright.

JIM. I went down Fifty-Seven Street last night.

SAM. Uh huh. And how was that?

JIM. Yeah. You know. Down on Fifty-Eight Street there.

SAM. Uh huh. You have a good time?

JIM. Yeah.

SAM. Uh huh.

49

JIM. Yeah. I was glad to be there.

SAM. I bet that you were. (*Miller and Fox enter.*)

MILLER. They make me tired and after a point I can't say I blame them.

SAM. Yessir. You get up there.

MILLER. (*Referring to Fox.*) Me and my man here both.

FOX. No. I don't need a shine.

MILLER. Come on, now, let me get you.

FOX. No, I got shined up yesterday.

SAM. We gonna get you now. (*Miller and Fox climb up on the shoeshine stand.*)

FOX. (*Waving Sam off.*) I'm alright.

SAM. (*Starting on Miller.*) Yessuh! (*Pause.*)

JIM. (*Of shoes.*) Sucker dropped these in the *mud* . . . (*Miller sighs loudly.*)

FOX. Uh huh. (*Pause.*)

MILLER. The whole thing.

FOX. Yeah.

SAM. You got some salt here.

MILLER. Uh huh. (*Pause.*)

SAM. You want me to take it off?

MILLER. What do you use to get it off?

SAM. What? (*Pause.*)

MILLER. What do you use to get the salt off?

JIM. . . . Down on Fifty-*Eight* Street.

SAM. Don't you worry now. We get it off.

MILLER. (*To Fox.*) You got 'em shined up yesterday.

FOX. Uh huh. (*Pause.*)

MILLER. Hmm. (*Fox picks up a newspaper.*)

SAM. Yessir. You take that paper. That's for you.

JIM. Want me to do these clear ones?

SAM. Yeah. You do them with the saddle soap.

MILLER. (*To Fox of paper.*) What's in there?

FOX. Nothing. (*Pause.*)

MILLER. You go down to Intercorp?

FOX. No.

MILLER. John Reynolds saw you down there.

FOX. Well, I only stopped by.

MILLER. Why?

FOX. You know.

MILLER. No.

50

FOX. To talk to some people.

MILLER. Uh huh. Yeah. I wouldn't take it, you know.

FOX. No?

MILLER. Uh uh. They offered it to me.

FOX. I wish they'd offered it to me.

MILLER. You'd be a fool to talk to them. I think you'd be a fool to go in there.

FOX. Come on, I only went down to say hello.

JIM. . . . The *saddle* soap.

MILLER. And how is everyone down there?

FOX. Fine. (*Dowd enters.*)

SAM. (*To Dowd.*) Yessuh. Did you forget something?

DOWD. I think I lost my wallet here.

MILLER. I saw where Charlie Beeman's moved.

FOX. Where were you sitting?

DOWD. Up there. (*Miller and Fox search for the wallet. Pause.*)

FOX. It isn't here.

MILLER. How long ago'd you . . .

DOWD. Just a minute . . .

SAM. Just before you came.

MILLER. Huh! (*Pause.*)

DOWD. None of you saw a wallet here?

MILLER. No.

SAM. Jimmy . . . ?

FOX. No.

JIM. What?

SAM. You seen a wallet?

JIM. No. (*Pause.*)

SAM. I'm sorry, mister.

JIM. . . . What? I seen a *wallet*?

SAM. Yeah.

JIM. No. (*Pause.*)

SAM. I'm sorry, mister. (*Pause.*) You can look around. Ain't no one moved since you left.

DOWD. Could I talk to you? (*Starts taking Sam aside.*)

SAM. Uh?

DOWD. Please, one moment. (*Takes him aside.*)

MILLER. Uh, buddy, can your friend finish me up?

SAM. Jim, you finish up that man. (*Jim goes to do so.*)

DOWD. Now, I had a lot of   MILLER. I knew him back at

money, I just cashed a
check, and . . .
SAM. Mister, I swear on my
life . . .
DOWD. No, wait a second.

C&D, you know?
FOX. Yeah?
MILLER. Oh *yeah*. Son of a
bitch then . . .
FOX. Uh huh.

JIM. You using the saddle soap on these?
SAM. Yes. I am.
JIM. Alright.
MILLER. You'll finish off the bottoms with the brown . . . ?
JIM. Sure will.

DOWD. Listen to me; I'd
hate to have to *do* anything
about this.
SAM. Do what you want, we
didn't find your billfold here.
DOWD. It's not the money,
do you understand?

MILLER. I mean, you want
to spend your time in office
politics you're going to rise.
FOX. Uh huh.

MILLER. You want to *do* it
that way.
FOX. Yeah.

SAM. I understand it all. I just can't help you.
DOWD. I would hate to have to go and get the cops.
SAM. Mister, you trace your steps back. *I* don't know . . .
MILLER. Where were you before you were here?
DOWD. Next door.
MILLER. (*To Fox.*) . . . You want to brown-nose your way
through *life* . . .

DOWD. (*To Sam.*) Look,
look, I'll give you one-third
of the money if I get the
wallet back. (*Pause.*)
. . . With all the cards.

MILLER. . . . If you're con-
tent to live your life like that.
I told him one day, "I'm a
maverick, Charl, I can't live
life your way. I got to go out
there. You don't have to
go in the houses."

JIM. How much was in it?
DOWD. Did you take it?
JIM. No.

FOX. Yeah.
MILLER. *Huh*?

DOWD. Then what the fuck business do you have asking how
much was in it?
SAM. You go an' call your cops.
MILLER. I mean if you want to get *Byzantine* . . .

52

JIM. I was just asking, sucker.

DOWD. You've got no business to know.

JIM. I don't?

DOWD. You absolutely don't.

JIM. Unless I took it.

DOWD. Uh huh, yeah.

JIM. An' then I *know* how much it was.

DOWD. That's right.

JIM. So what the fuck I'm *asking* for? You motherfucker, get out of this store.

DOWD. I don't want to come back here with the police . . .

SAM. You come back however you want. Now we don't have your money. If we had it we would give it to you. (*Pause. Dowd exits.*) Oooeee! Now there's a fellow that was *mad* . . .

JIM. . . . Sonofabitch . . .

SAM. That sucker's *mad* . . .	MILLER. I mean, if you want
JIM. . . . Come in here like	to brown-nose your way
the viceroy of some place.	through life. It isn't worth it.
	Fuck it.
	FOX. Yeah.

SAM. Sucker come in here yesterday . . .

JIM. Yeah . . .

SAM. Me an Bill here, he say, "Which one of you fellows going to give me a fine *shine* today?"

MILLER. You're going to do that brown thing?

JIM. Yeah. I'll do her.

MILLER. In fifty years who's going to know who went to Maui with the boss.

SAM. "Which one o' you fellows going to give me a *shoeshine* to-day!"

JIM. Hnuh!

MILLER. . . . They wonder why the people walk.

FOX. Uh huh.

SAM. "Get up," Bill say, "You want your shoes shined you get up there."

MILLER. . . . Not one word of backing.

FOX. No.

JIM. He get up?

SAM. Yeah. He got up there.

MILLER. I'm sorry . . .

JIM. . . . Sonofabitch.

MILLER. . . . Buddy up to you at Christmas if you made the list . . .

SAM. "Which one you mens goan shine my nice sweet shoes today . . ."

MILLER. He wants his picture with his arm around you in the Trades . . .

JIM. . . . Sonofabitch.

MILLER. And if you didn't make the list that year, fuck you.

FOX. Uh huh.

MILLER. I'm glad that sucker's gone.

JIM. (*Of nothing in particular.*) Yessuh . . .

MILLER. I'll live without him very well.

SAM. How late you stayin' in?

JIM. How late you need me?

SAM. Can you stay 'til six?

MILLER. How is he looking?

FOX. Fine.

JIM. You need me?

SAM. Yeah.

JIM. Alright.

MILLER. I'll bet he is.

JIM. You done.

MILLER. (*Rising.*) What do I owe you?

JIM. Dollar.

MILLER. . . . Gone to fucking *Maui* every goddam month . . . how much?

JIM. One dollar. (*Pause.*)

MILLER. A dollar for a shine?

JIM. Yessuh! (*Pause.*) Thass a *spit* shine! (*Pause. Miller digs in his pocket and starts to pay.*)

MILLER. (*To Sam.*) Did you find that guy's wallet?

SAM. Shit. No sir. You have a good day now.

MILLER. (*Exiting, to Fox.*) Yeah. I heard you went down there. . .

SAM. How much he give you?

JIM. Twenny cent.

SAM. Sonofabitch . . . (*Pause. Jim goes back to work on uninhabited shoes.*)

JIM. Yeah. They was down on Fifty-Seven Street down there.

SAM. Who?

JIM. *You* know. Richard . . . everybody . . .

SAM. Uh huh.

JIM. This stuff don't come off.

SAM. You use some Brillo on it?

JIM. That won't help.

SAM. No?

JIM. Uh uh. (*Pause.*)

SAM. You try it.

JIM. I will.

SAM. Did you find that fellow's billfold?

JIM. Shit.

SAM. Well did you? (*Customer enters.*)

CUSTOMER. Shoeshine.

SAM. You get up there! (*Customer takes seat, picks up paper.*) Yessuh. Thass right. Thass for you! (*Starts on shoes. To Jim.*) 'Cause if you found that thing you best had tell me.

JIM. No, I didn't find nothin'.

CUSTOMER. What did you lose?

SAM. He lost his wallet somewhere in here

CUSTOMER. (*Producing cigarette.*) Do you have a match?

SAM. Yessuh, I surely do. (*Lights Customer's cigarette. Pause. To Jim.*) 'Cause you know if I found it I'd tell you.

JIM. I know you would.

SAM. You know I would.

CUSTOMER. I got a spot of paint or something on the toe.

SAM. Yessuh, I see it.

JIM. . . . Yeah, they was all down there drinkin' . . .

SAM. Uh huh. If them people come back here, you best had tell the truth.

JIM. I told the truth.

SAM. Uh huh.

JIM. I tole the truth.

SAM. We gonna see.

JIM. Well man I tole you what the truth was, so you just think what you want.

SAM. I will.

JIM. How late you say you want me to stay today?

SAM. Thass up to you — I'm stayin' to six.

JIM. I'll stay too.

SAM. Yeah, you do what you want.

JIM. Shit.

55

SAM. Fine pair of shoes you got here.

CUSTOMER. Thank you.

JIM. I'm gettin' to the red.

SAM. You call me 'fore you do 'em.

JIM. Yes I will. (*To self.*) . . . She said we fucked 'em up . . .

SAM. Huh?

JIM. Yeah. I'm glad I wasn't here.

SAM. Well, don't you worry. She be back.

JIM. Uh huh. (*Pause.*) How I know *you* didn't find it.

SAM. Shit, I found it man, how come I'm askin' you?

JIM. Uh huh.

PROPERTY PLOT

ON STAGE:
Brown boots, red boots, other pairs of boots and shoes ticketed for shoeshining

Shoeshine stand, newspaper

Saddle soap, Brillo, shoeshine cloths, etc.

PERSONAL:
Cigarettes (Sam)

Money (Miller)

Cigarettes (Customer)

Matches (Sam)

Litko: A Dramatic Monologue

LITKO was written as a companion piece for *The Duck Variations* in its 1973 Chicago premiere at the Body Politic. It featured Jim Brett, and was directed by the author.

CHARACTER

LITKO

Litko: A Dramatic Monologue

LITKO. (At rise Litko is discovered addressing the audience. Litko speaks.) Do we understand each other?

His demeanor and, in fact, his line ("Do we understand each other?") go far in helping to create a bond between Litko and his audience. Unbutton coat. Litko speaks: Let us dispense with formality, and get down to theatrical cliches.

The audience smiles appreciatively at his candid behavior.

Thanks, gang. Pause.

"I wonder if they realize the technical proficiency and purely traditional dramatic training necessary to establish the actor's comfort in a setting ostensibly devoid of qualities." Paper, mister?

"You can't go out there, Litko," he says to the audience. "Billy Brenner and the *Lazy 'J'* boys'll cut you down like a muskrat." Many members of the audience wonder if they really know what a muskrat is. Litko assures them it is not important. "It is not important." That's easy for him to say.

A pause (*or silence*) ensues, broken only by sporadic coughing and the line "broken only by sporadic coughing and the line."

It becomes obvious to both parties to the theatrical *event* that a crux has been reached. Progression of some sort is clearly indicated.

A new character seems unlikely.

Introduction of further vocabulary is certainly within the limits of accepted tradition.

The appearance of a goofy prop or two . . . (don't hold your breath).

The re-occurrence of World War One . . . ?

Police brutality?

The news that some wild animal has escaped from a nearby zoo, and is believed hiding *right here in this theater!* (I'm spelling that "E," "R.") (At this point I shall go and look—or pretend to look—you're grownups, judge for yourselves—at several places

61

around the stage where this alleged animal might hide.) (But Litko does not move.) Which might just raise a question as to the responsibility of the dramatic artist to his audience. (What sophistry!) I will now deliver myself of the following: one of a number of previously prepared and memorized speeches:

"I love you. I have always loved you. I shall love you as long as there courses in my veins—and, to be realistic, in *your* veins—blood." Let us recapitulate. (Why? because it *feels* so good.) A while ago a person unknown to you . . .

"Of course," Litko allows, "some of you," addressing the audience directly—what high style!—"do know this person," indicating himself, "in another guise, or in different guises. But," he says, "I sincerely hope," leaving for the audience to decide for itself or themselves the veracity of the aforementioned hope, and whether the said hope is that of the character (that is to say, the *playwright*) or of the actor; and, if *of* the actor, of him truly, or but under the somewhat—let us face the facts—extenuating circumstances in which we now find him, and, just a bit further, if we really got the time for this diversion . . .

"I sincerely hope . . . " or, from another tack:

"In response to a tacit yet undeniable inquiry into the sincerity of my hope . . . " and

"As to the current employment of that which, believe me, can be taken as my true capacity for sincerity . . . " let us leave no stone unturned, though: "For those who desire the identity of him the sincerity of whose hope has, of late, so clearly manifest itself, let me reply." (No one indicates a reluctance to let him reply.)

Litko confronts his audience: "Hi, gang."

Some, apparently would appreciate a reply. Or do not care. Or are asleep.

Is a show of hands indicated? (In certain circumstances, yes.)

Why, then, does Litko not reply?

Has he been "struck dumb"?

Shall he lapse into song? Or dance? Or mixed-media? Or some more purely visual form of art? Has he the training? Has he the inclination? Has he the time? Is God dead? (No, I know, that's nothing to joke about.) This is no life for a grown man, Litko says, on the verge of great frenzy. (Emotion is freeing to look at, but tiresome to indulge in.) "A funny thing happened to me," Litko says, humor dripping from each word and gesture.

"Really now, seriously, folks, I have the sorry task of inform-
ing you that — yes, you guessed it — the theatre is dead" (Oh no.)
    — innocence, your eight-year-old foster child, Scooter, along
with a busload of his classmates enroute to the zoo, Beethoven,
LaFollette, and countless other individuals and institutions of
varying worth." (All of this, of course, having taken place over a
period of years, and astonishing only in the aggregate.)
    "What can we salvage of this carnage?" Litko asks, imaginary
tears coursing down his all-too-real cheeks, "Hope for the
future? The odd wristwatch?"
    (Wait a second, please.)
    "How old are you, Trigger?"
    (While my imaginary horse is counting, folks, and in the final
seconds of our time together here I'd like to say, on behalf of
myself, the author, the director, our wonderful stagehands —
seriously, don't they do a great job? — our house crew, *their*
families, and the many, many men and women who provide
them with the services and goods so necessary for the support of
life: keep your pecker up.)

    Anybody out there from Kankakee!?

In Old Vermont

CHARACTERS

ROGER

MAUD

In Old Vermont

ROGER. Do you remember when we were in Vermont that time?

MAUD. Of course.

ROGER. Do you remember that?

MAUD. Yes. (*Pause.*) The sky.

ROGER. The sky. Yes.

MAUD. Cold. The cold. The evenings. Sitting.

ROGER. "Old, old, old New England."

MAUD. Fire.

ROGER. The fire. Oh, yes.

MAUD. I like the mornings. Do you know why?

ROGER. Why?

MAUD. It will become warm.

Also, in the evenings. When the sun goes down. In afternoons.

In winter. When the sun goes down.

It becomes warm. In afternoon. The sun shines.

All the snow is bright.

The cold protects us.

It can warm us.

In the winter.

In the snow.

Like skating on the ice.

The shock comes.

With the fissure. Falling. (*Pause.*)

For moments.

For one moment. When you know that you are cold. (*Pause.*)

Then it seeps in.

When the cold comes it is warm.

As if you'd wet the bed.

The rabbits turn. They turn to white.

I like it in the winter. For we . . . For we are *protected.* (*Pause.*)

You hear?

THEN WE ARE ALONE!

IN A VACATION HOME. WE'RE WAITING!
FOR THE *WHAT*? THE SPIRIT.
Indians could come. Where would we hide? Where would we
go then? We'd not made provisions. It is much too late.
We could have cut a cellar in the ground or made a secret room
between the logs, or in the roof.
A deep, deep cellar down. Beneath the rug. *They'd* never find it!
Do not tell me that. Not if you tamped it down. Not if you
tamped the dirt down. *Trampled* it and fit the logs in. Covered
with an Oriental rug in red.
They'd stomp, they'd stomp, they'd all try to search out our
hiding place.
But they could not. They couldn't *find* it.
So don't tell me that.
If we had built it. If we'd built it. If we'd took the time.
But no!
The shock of when they come.
The tommyhawk.
The genitals hacked off.
The cold and roasting flesh.
Your own hands severed and your eyes like boils.
Like fevered boils, like ponds. Like flying geese.
Our screams mean nothing.
Far above the summer scene.
The hot. The sickly heat.
The fire. Burning down.
The wings.
The flapping of the windowshade.
The upturned lamp.
A candle guttered.
Someone finds a bag of salt.
That they had overturned.
(*A long pause.*)
In old Vermont.

All Men Are Whores

ALL MEN ARE WHORES was first presented in February, 1977 at the Yale Cabaret.

The Cast was: Patti LuPone
Kevin Kline
Sam Tsoutsovas

The production was directed by the author.

All Men Are Whores

ONE

SAM. Our concept of time is predicated upon our understanding of death.

Time passes solely because death ends time. Our understanding of death is arrived at, in the main, because of the nature of sexual reproduction.

Organisms which reproduce through fission do not "die."

The stream of life, the continuation of the germ plasm, is unbroken.

Clearly.

Just as it is in the case of man.

But much less apparently so in our case. For we are sentient. We are conscious of ourselves, and conscious of the schism in our sexuality.

And so we perceive time. (*Pause.*) And so we will do anything for some affection.

TWO

KEVIN. I saw her in the Art Institute four years ago. I saw her from the back, her neck, she sat up. Near the Oriental art. The horses. She faced down away from me her hair was dark, she had a cotton suit on.

I looked at her a long time at her back. I thought that if you walk away from her you'll always wish you had (I knew that I would think about her).

In the way she faced away from me I couldn't see her.

I went over to the case in front of her. (*Pause.*)

She had been out in the sun.

Hello. She looked at me. I stood there. I saw that she was reading she had put her book aside.

A long time. (*Pause.*)

She put her hand on my arm she smelled, I don't know, like musk, faint brushing hair on her neck, back, wisps. . . .

Slowly, in the cloakroom, in the hall I said that I just live a little way from here.

She put her head down on my shoulder in the taxicab, I wondered how can someone be so light, she took my chin and kissed me, she put my hand underneath her dress and rubbed my hand against her.

I just live on the second floor, she nodded, we went up.

I took her jacket, take me in the bedroom, she said.

She was like an otter, she was sleek. (*Pause.*)

I'm glad we met, I said, you make me feel good.

What, was I asleep, she said? (*Pause.*)

Please. What time is it?

I helped her find her things I took her face to kiss her. Please, I have to go, she told me.

Are You married, I said, no. Oh. Will you call me?

Yes.

You have the number?

Are you in the book, she said? (*Pause.*)

Yes.

Good . . . (*Pause.*)

When I saw her on the bus a month ago, Hello, I said. I'll bet that you don't remember me. (*Pause.*)

Have you been here this whole time? (*Pause.*) Have you been here all this time?

THREE

SAM. If we could reproduce like paramecia do you think that we would not?

When the secrets of the age were clear to him he took it like a man, which is to say as one who has no choice.

FOUR

PATTI. He said he thought of me with great affection, still. He had this fantasy where he came over and he knew something was wrong, he came in I was in the kitchen here there was this huge, ah, I don't know, a maniac, he'd hurt me, he had hurt my face, he bruised me, I had bruises on my breasts, I had become all helpless, I thought I was going to die and I was whimpering when he came in he saw what the man was doing, and he filled with rage he tore him off of me and threw him on the floor and killed him.

He says, "You should not be let to live," he did vile things to him, I don't know, he kicked him in the testicles, or put his eyes out. (*Pause.*)

Because he'd hurt me and this filled him with such rage the man should not be let to live. Because he thought of me with great affection still.

FIVE

KEVIN. Oh. (*Pause.*) Those cool forearms on my shoulder.
Her blue shirt was tied around her waist.
I licked her armpits.
Sweat. Her shirt. She kept her shirt on, I unbuttoned it and kissed her breasts. (Our bellies got so slippery.)
That morning, when we woke up, at the sink, her pants, her cotton pants, she washed her hair out at the sink, and when she took her shirt off I came up behind and held onto her breasts and she told me to wait, she would be done, wait, when she got the soap off.
We sat on the porch. (*Pause.*) Please make love to me.
Please tell me that you'd like for me to do things to you.
In my dream I dreamt you would. (*Pause.*) I always dreamt you would. I knew you would.

73

SIX

SAM. I like a nice ass.
I like a nice ass and legs. (*Pause.*)
The ass is the top of the legs.

SEVEN

PATTI. He said that what he thought that beauty was, that *beauty* was the striving, the unconscious striving of the germ plasm to find a mate who would, when coupled with itself, improve the race. (*Pause.*)
He thought that those things we found beautiful were those which would improve the race. (Is that right? Yes. Alright.)
So. What, I said, big titties and firm thighs and things for bearing in the fields? Right? He told me no. That we were overpopulated and we now need something else.
And those things which we need form our ideas of what's beautiful.
Oh. Yes, I said, I see: conditioning. Ideas someone places in your mind. Like advertising. No, he said. You cannot step outside the culture: Those who educate you, someone taught them, too.
You see?
I did not see, no, but this turned me on. Please kiss me, I said.
They were educated, too, he said. (No, wait.)
(Alright.)
We strive . . . we strive . . .
To *what*, I said?
We strive . . . our loins . . . we're driven . . . (As a race, I said, or individuals?)
A race.
(A woman of my age would never ask a man to her apartment for an after-dinner drink unless she wanted him. He surely knows this.)
Wait, do you like Tolstoy, he said?
No. I do not like Tolstoy.
No? Why?

Oh. (*Sighs.*) I don't know.

Many reasons— (*Pause.*)

We find those things beautiful, he said, we feel may improve us. (Our unconscious longings.)

(I was wet, but now I'm not.)

Yes. Do you read a lot, he asked me?

Yes. I read.

Oh, really, what?

Things. Books.

A long pause came here. You have lovely eyes he said. (*Pause.*)

Thank you.

Yes. He said. I like your breasts. Thank you, I said, they're rather small.

I like that, he said. Do you? Yes.

I ran my right hand through his hair.

He sat there for a moment then moved by me on the couch.

Uh . . . *listen*, he said . . .

Yes?

EIGHT

KEVIN. I hate your family.

You know, I think there *are* no interesting restaurants.

She would suck me off in taxicabs. (I feel she would.)

I think a man could lose his life with her.

OFFSTAGE VOICE. Our small cabals.

KEVIN. I think her fingers taste of gun oil.

OFFSTAGE VOICE. Jive mesmery of musk and fish . . .

KEVIN. I think she smells like musk and cordite. We should be down in the West Side by the docks with browning automatics. She's a cannibal and who the fuck knows *what* she does. (*Pause.*) Who have *you* killed?

Eh? When they drop the atom bomb, are you going to make me *soup*????

I want to see tattoos, and fuck you with your eyeshadow.

I mean it.

OFFSTAGE VOICE. Harlotry and necromancy. (*Pause.*)

KEVIN. I mean it.

75

NINE

PATTI. I want to tie you to the bed, he said.
Okay, I said.
I want to lick all over you he said, I told him yes, I'd like that.
Would you. Yes. I said.
I want to chain you face down and to bite you all around your pussy.
Okay, I told him. Don't hurt me, though.
He said he wouldn't, but he asked me could he be a little rough.
I told him sure, just if he didn't hurt me.
He told me that he might just have to be a little rough.
Don't be too rough, I asked him, and he said he'd try not to, but sometimes he thought that it was a good idea for someone to be rough.
Alright, I said, just so long as they are gentle, too. It doesn't matter what you called it just so long as you don't hurt another person.
No, he said, but sometimes just a little pain could be erotic. Did I think so?
I told him what? What do you mean? You tell me what you want to do, whatever, it's okay or not, but we can talk about it. I want you to feel good and I want to feel good, too, I want to get out, too, to get off.
You know that I like you.
I told you I like you.
Take your clothes off, he said. Okay, I said.
Now, he told me. Okay, I said, you take yours off, too.
No, he said, I only want to watch, okay.
He told me that he thought I have a lovely body, which was nice.
I told him he should take his clothes off and he sad, alright, that he would in a minute.
It's alright, I told him. It's alright.
I want to hit you, he said. No, you don't, I said.
I *do*, though, he said.
No, you don't I said. You know you don't.
I *do*, though, he said.
No, you don't. Come here. Come here. And then I, him, we went, over to the couch and sat down there and I held him a while, we sat there, and I got the blanket later on and put it over us and fell asleep.

TEN

SAM. At the Art Institute. The French Impressionists.
Some salesman from Ohio.
I said, Hello, do you like Mary Cassatt?
He said he thought so, was this one of hers.
I looked. Yes.
He sat. We talked.
He comes in every two weeks. For some company.
I smiled. Let's take a walk.
Oh, he said, sure, if you don't mind. I'd like to see the North
Side.
We walked by the lake, down by the Yacht Club (he'd been in
the Navy).
Such a fine day . . .
We went back to my . . . he said Oh, do you *live* around
here . . . ? my apartment and we drank a bit.
He told me that the kind (that he was looking) that the sort of a
relationship that he was looking for would take a long, long time
to, I don't know, to ferment. He said that he thought that
people shouldn't go to bed together for some (a certain)
measured time, a month, three months . . . in which to get to
know each other well.
He told me that he wanted to be friends with me. He felt we
could be close. (These things take time.) Eleven thirty.
I said, my friend, look: you think (you may think . . .) you want
some lasting . . . *I* don't know . . . some lasting something.
(Nothing lasts forever . . .) (I don't know what it is that you
want.) But now, tonight, for my *own* self, what I want is to get
laid. Thank you. Call me.
Then I took a shower and went out.

ELEVEN

KEVIN. It seemed I had discovered a capacity for being happy
with a woman.
When my possession of this talent had occurred to me I rejoiced
that I would not be lonely anymore, but move from one affair to

yet another learning from each woman with whom I spent time, and living through the periods of my romantic re-alignments with both grace and happy resignation.

Lately, though, I find I am confused. I realize, I think, that one can only learn from these encounters if one makes some sort of compact with the person with whom one is spending time. (*Pause.*)

These contracts, these avowals of desire, of (let us face the facts) *compulsion*. (*Pause.*) They may *increase* desire (or our capacity for such) but limit our ability to act with our new-found and *profound* emotional resources. (*Pause.*)

How can this end, other than in great resentment of one's current partner? (*Pause.*)

Quite frankly, how?

TWELVE

PATTI. We built our fires on the beach, and every night we sat by them and talked and ate our food, and we made love and slept.

As fall came we moved back into the dunes. (*Pause.*)

Later, we went further. To the woods; but walked or fished or searched for clams or driftwood in the mornings and the afternoons. And as we walked we saw the charred-out fires we had built, each in a different place, and said "do you remember that night?" (*Pause.*)

"The night we had that fire? What we ate, and how we touched each other? (*Pause.*) Do you remember." (*Pause.*)

Or later, walking in the dunes I'd come across a hill into a gully when the sand had blown — the place was changed, of course, but something still remained. The logs, the angles they had fallen in . . . It wouldn't be the same when spring came. Traces of our camp would be obliterated by the winter and the shore itself would change. (We thought as we lived back in the trees.) (*Pause.*)

Where we moved back. (*Pause.*)

Where we retired.(*Pause.*)

"Do you remember that night?" we would say . . .

THIRTEEN

SAM. Where were you? You weren't there. You know what it means to me when you're late. There's going to come a time when this is life and death, these assignations.
You never fulfill my instructions. You don't.
Do you think that I *care*?
Do you know what I care about? *Loyalty*.
Do you think that I care for six *minutes*?
Eh? What do you think I *am*? Don't you *see* . . . ? There's going to come a time when this is life and *death*.
There are things going on, there are things going on in this country you cannot be imprecise. You can*not* . . . ! (*Pause.*)
And it just takes you ages to leave anywhere. (And you can't keep your fucking mouth shut.) Do you think that I care for *appearances*? What I care for (what I care for miss) (yes) is *survival. Survival.*
(You're so secure . . .)
What do you know? You don't know what life is. You know *nothing*.

FOURTEEN

KEVIN. He brought the coffee, it was very good. I lit a cigarette, I looked at her. She smiled.
I have something for you, she said.
Oh, what?
A thing . . . something. She took a package from her purse, she gave it to me. She smiled.
Shall I open it? Yes, open it.
She's bought me a gold lighter. (*Pause.*)
It's lovely, I said. (*Pause.*) You shouldn't have.
She'd had it engraved with my name. And then " I love you," and her name. It's lovely, I said.
Do you like it?
Yes, I said, you shouldn't have.
She smiled. (*Pause.*) You don't like it.
No, I like it very much, it's lovely.
No. You don't.

79

I do.

No.

Yes, I do, I told her. (*Pause.*) You shouldn't have though.

No? (*Pause.*) Why? (*Pause.*) Why? (*Pause.*)

Look, I told her. We are friends (are we friends?).

What do you mean "friends?" What?

We are friends, I want to be your friend, I said. (*Pause.*)

What does this mean, she asked me.

Please, not now, I said.

No. Now. Now, please, what does this mean? (*Pause.*)

Look, I told her.

No, she said. Don't tell me this, (*Pause.*) No, don't do this.

Keep your voice down.

I don't care. (*Pause.*) *I* don't care . . .

He came back and he stopped and asked if we'd like some more coffee . . .

No, she said, don't tell me this. (*Pause.*) No. She started crying. Are you alright, I said? What? (*Pause.*) No. Would you like something? Something? *What?* I don't know, can I get you something? (Do we have to do this here?) (*Pause.*) Would you like to leave? (*Pause.*) Shall we leave?

Leave me alone. She got up, he came over to pull out her chair but she was gone. I sat there. (*Pause.*)

He asked me if I'd care for something else. (*Pause.*) Some more coffee . . . (*Pause.*) What? No. (*Pause.*) Yes.

"I love you." (*Pause.*) I lit a cigarette.

FIFTEEN

PATTI. Come here come here.

I know what you want.

You don't have to say it.

I know.

You don't have to say you want it.

I know.

I know; you don't want it. I know.

But come here.

It's alright.

I'm here.

80

Come on.
No.
Come on.
Yes.
Come here.
You lie down, now.
That's alright.
You lie down.
Good.
That's good.
Good.
Now be quiet. You be quiet now.
I know.
Now I am going to make you feel good.
I know.
You be quiet, now. That's alright.
I know what you want. (*Pause.*)
You don't have to tell me that you want it.
That's alright.
You just be still now.
That's alright. (*Pause.*)
Good.

SIXTEEN

SAM. The problems of the universe. We are programmed to
love our loved ones, all our paramours, our wives, our
husbands. (*Pause.*) We are programmed to love our race. To
help our race survive.
This is a chemic fiat, and what does it have, I ask you, what, to
do with metaphysics? Neither *are* there metaphysics, no. But
only more increasingly occult degrees of understanding—hid-
den, though, only because of our interminable arrogance—Our
race-conceit. (Is this true?) We are the stuff that rocks are made
of and cannot be broken of the habit of an intuition of some
specialness— (*Pause.*)
We are the fish.
When it all comes to chemicals.

Where are our mothers, now? Where are they? In the moment of our death, or birth, of orgasm or hunger?
When it all comes down to carbon, or to hydrogen?
In cities where we kill for comfort—for a moment of reprieve from our adulterated lives—for fellow-feeling. (*Pause.*)
(I have eyelashes, too . . .)
Some night when you have been up half the night alone when you have read instructions on the phonebook, eh?
Then, when the walls scream. Eh?
Who'd sell our souls just to be ratified, in taxicabs, in some resort, along the cradle, by a touch (a friend, our mother . . .) who would make the world go. (*Pause.*)
One moment of release.
Psychic reprieve.
(Oh,God, what are we doing here?)
We are uprooted.
We have no connection. (*Pause.*)
We beat each other by the docks or dressed in jackboots and in uniforms, and preen in passing windows just like everyone.
Our life is garbage.
We take comfort in our work and cruelty. We love the manicurist and the nurse for they hold hands with us. Where is our mother now? We woo with condoms and a ferry ride; the world around us crumples into chemicals, we stand intractable, and wait for someone competent to take us 'cross the street. (*Pause.*)
Where are our preceptors now? Or at the moment of death, and would *you* not do all you can, forsaking anything, for one swift moment of surcease? (The bettered bodies, news photographers, pulp analyses, (*Pause.*) crimson sheets . . .)
My god, we've done what we should not have. (*Pause.*)
I'm sure we must have.

SEVENTEEN

PATTI. We wait for someone—
KEVIN. Tie me up and beat me.
PATTI. Look, I told him, look, what do I care if I am right for you or not (for me or not) (if you are . . . ?).

82

All I only care is do I want to be with you (because I want to be with you) and that you make me happy.

KEVIN. Yes, I swear to God that if I have to spend another Sunday evening by myself that I am going to blow my brains out.

PATTI. Look:

KEVIN. Now is this so unreasonable?

SAM. Precious anomalies of lovers' flesh, quirks of behavior, heartbreaking inside curves of thigh. (*Pause.*) The curriculum of small cabals that we endeavor to create or to prolong . . .

PATTI. (Don't stop . . .)

SAM. . . . The search for an exclusive union redolent of saltwater and gun-oil; alcohol on cotton balls after tattooing, soap, and liquid-paper . . .

KEVIN. Individuating qualities.

Like fires burnt out on the beach.

SAM. (The orthographical misjudgments in her love letters . . .)

PATTI. (*Pause.*) Yes.

SAM. Our small cabals. (*Pause.*) And why not?

KEVIN. Secret moon-borne signals are denied us, and we spill our seed upon the ground. (*Pause.*)

At the moment of our death we still embrace catholicism or the flag or. reach for our executors. (*Pause.*)

Our great epiphany by some bizarre concidence comes at the moment of our death.

SAM. When they get deep. (*Pause.*) Women, when they moan, they go nuts and their voices get deep. They are saying "look (I think) this is not what you think it is," they're saying "look." (*Pause.*)

KEVIN. So enthrall to that saline flesh.

SAM. (Yes.)

PATTI. We know the organism is by no means perfect. We can admit the possibility of some divine control (or absence of control). Of some Much Greater plan, or oversight. We recognize this in the body, we can see the flesh is far from perfect. We are the repositories of disease and physical disaster. This is patent, and we see that something is mistaken. (*Pause.*) What if this undignified and headlong thrusting toward each other's sex is nothing but an oversight or physical malformity? (*Pause.*) Should we not, perhaps retrain ourselves to revel in the sexual act not as the consummation of predestined and regenerate desire, but rather as a two-part affirmation of our need for solace in extremis.

KEVIN. (Goodnight.)

PATTI. In a world where nothing works.

SAM. No.

PATTI. In which we render extreme unction with our genitalia. (*Pause.*)